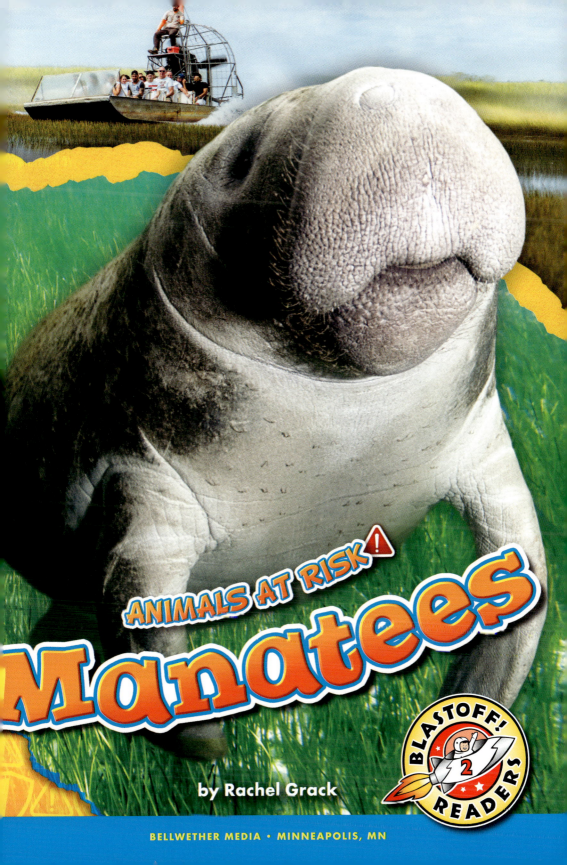

ANIMALS AT RISK
Manatees

by Rachel Grack

BLASTOFF! READERS 2

BELLWETHER MEDIA • MINNEAPOLIS, MN

Blastoff! Readers are carefully developed by literacy experts to build reading stamina and move students toward fluency by combining standards-based content with developmentally appropriate text.

Level 1 provides the most support through repetition of high-frequency words, light text, predictable sentence patterns, and strong visual support.

Level 2 offers early readers a bit more challenge through varied sentences, increased text load, and text-supportive special features.

Level 3 advances early-fluent readers toward fluency through increased text load, less reliance on photos, advancing concepts, longer sentences, and more complex special features.

★ **Blastoff! Universe**

Reading Level

Grade K

Grades 1–3

Grade 4

This edition first published in 2024 by Bellwether Media, Inc.

No part of this publication may be reproduced in whole or in part without written permission of the publisher. For information regarding permission, write to Bellwether Media, Inc., Attention: Permissions Department, 6012 Blue Circle Drive, Minnetonka, MN 55343.

Library of Congress Cataloging-in-Publication Data

Names: Koestler-Grack, Rachel A., 1973- author.
Title: Manatees / Rachel Grack.
Description: Minneapolis, MN : Bellwether Media, 2024. | Series: Blastoff! Readers. Animals at risk | Includes bibliographical references and index. | Audience: Ages 5-8 | Audience: Grades 2-3 | Summary: "Relevant images match informative text in this introduction to why manatees are at risk. Intended for students in kindergarten through third grade"-- Provided by publisher.
Identifiers: LCCN 2023004266 (print) | LCCN 2023004267 (ebook) | ISBN 9798886874204 (library binding) | ISBN 9798886876086 (ebook)
Subjects: LCSH: Manatees--Juvenile literature. | Manatees--Conservation--Juvenile literature.
Classification: LCC QL737.S63 K64 2024 (print) | LCC QL737.S63 (ebook) | DDC 599.55--dc23/eng/20230130
LC record available at https://lccn.loc.gov/2023004266
LC ebook record available at https://lccn.loc.gov/2023004267

Text copyright © 2024 by Bellwether Media, Inc. BLASTOFF! READERS and associated logos are trademarks and/or registered trademarks of Bellwether Media, Inc.

Editor: Kieran Downs   Designer: Brittany McIntosh

Printed in the United States of America, North Mankato, MN.

Table of Contents

Slow Swimmers	4
In Danger!	8
Save the Manatees!	12
Glossary	22
To Learn More	23
Index	24

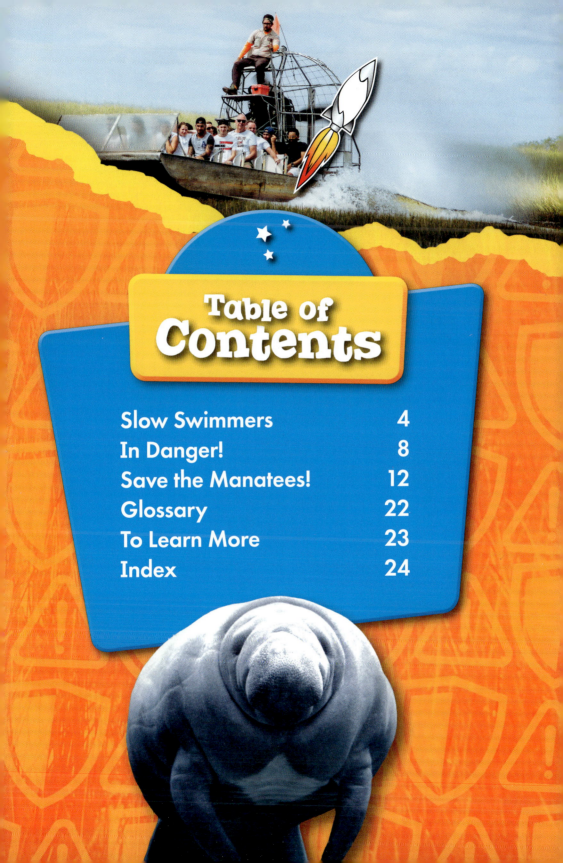

Slow Swimmers

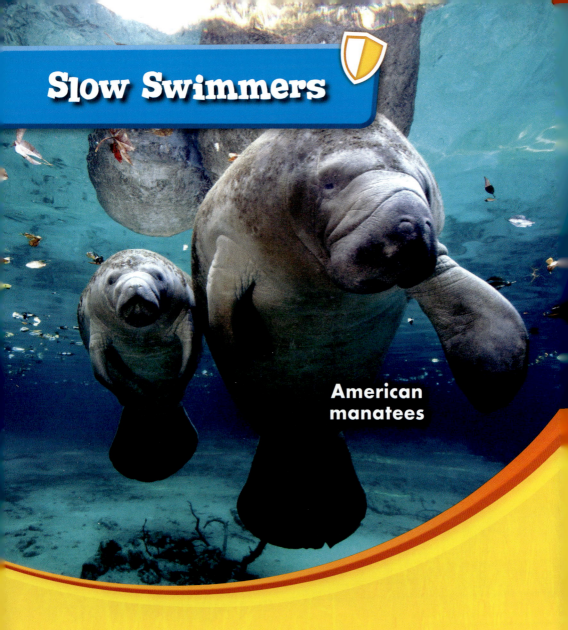

American manatees

Manatees are slow-moving sea **mammals**. They have large bodies and wide, whiskered noses.

There are three **species** of manatees. They all live in **shallow** waters.

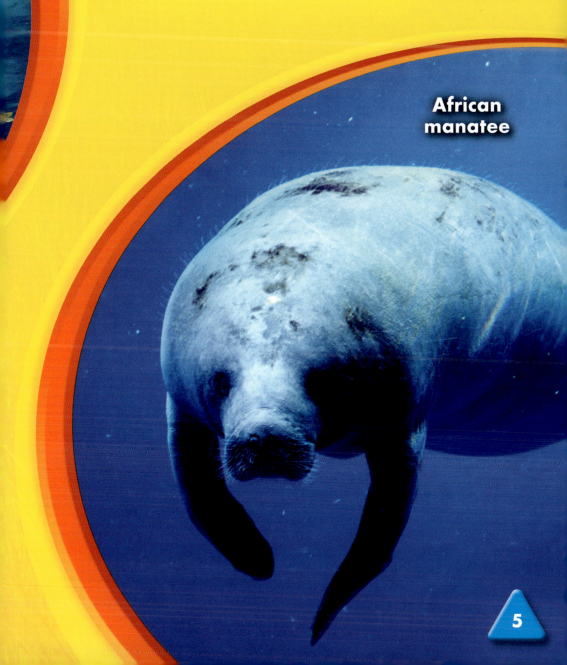

African manatee

Manatees find food and safety near **mangroves**. They swim in rivers and coastal wetlands.

But people are spreading into their **habitats**. Many manatees die every year.

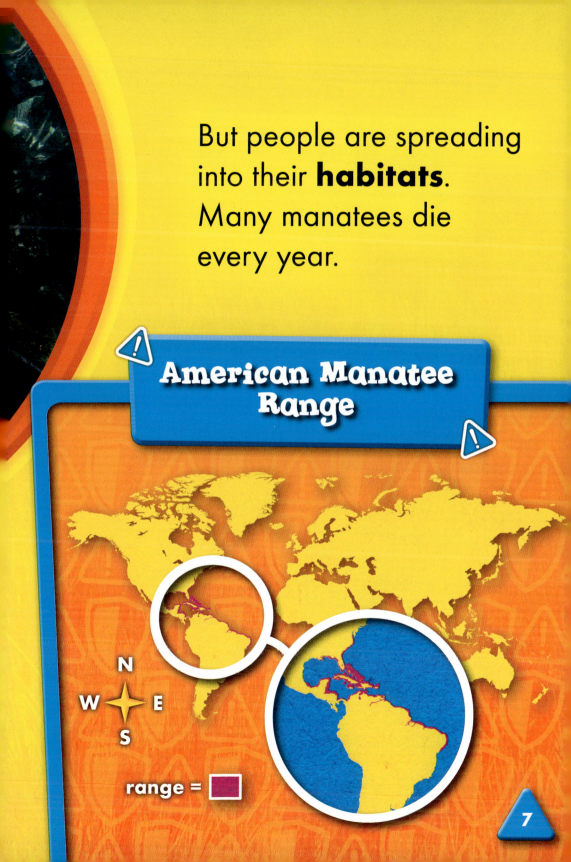

American Manatee Range

range =

In Danger!

seagrass

Manatees feed on seagrass along coasts. But people build along coasts. This hurts seagrass.

Climate change slows the growth of seagrass. Manatees have less to eat.

Threats

1. people build along coasts

2. seagrass is lost

3. manatees lose food

9

People fish in manatees' homes. Many manatees get caught in fishing nets. Others are hit by boats.

Pollution also hurts manatees. They can die from eating plastic.

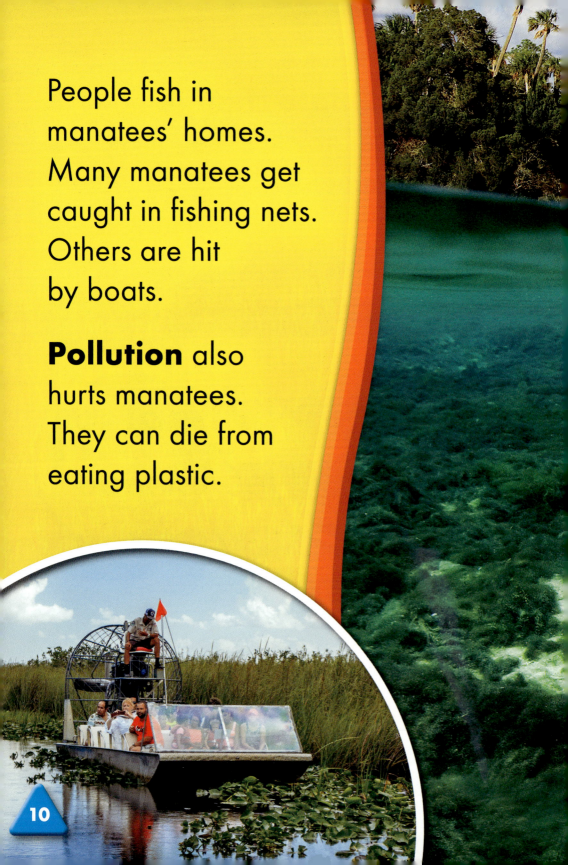

American Manatee Stats

| Least Concern | Near Threatened | **Vulnerable** | Endangered | Critically Endangered | Extinct in the Wild | Extinct |

conservation status: vulnerable

life span: up to 60 years

Save the Manatees!

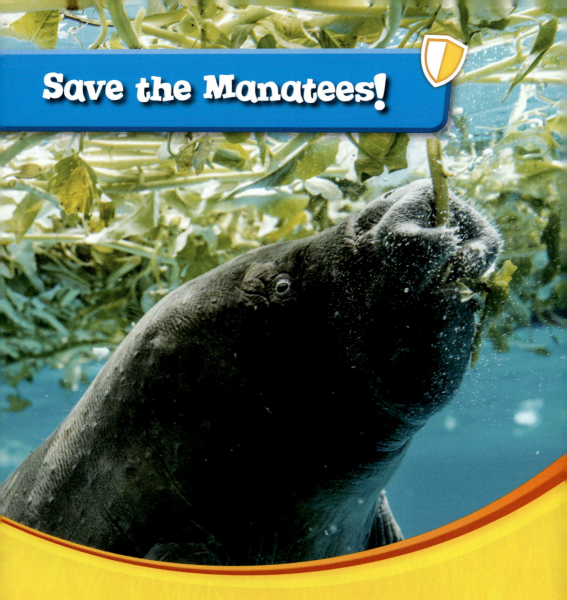

Manatees help their habitats. They eat plants that harm their homes. They keep seagrass short and healthy.

Without manatees, sea life would suffer.

The World with Manatees

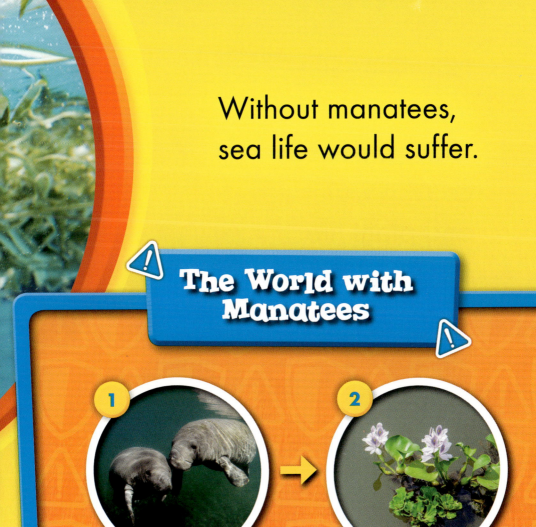

1. more manatees
2. fewer harmful plants
3. healthy habitats

People work to save manatee habitats. They **protect** coastal waters and plant life.

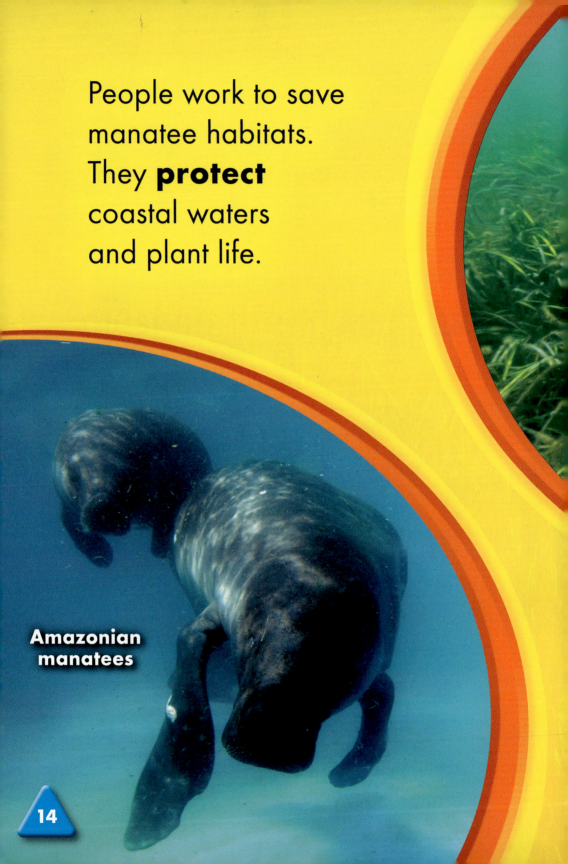

Amazonian manatees

They make sure seagrass growth stays healthy.

manatee refuge

Governments set up **refuges** for manatees. Protected areas allow manatees to travel safely.

Wildlife workers track manatees. They help manatees in danger.

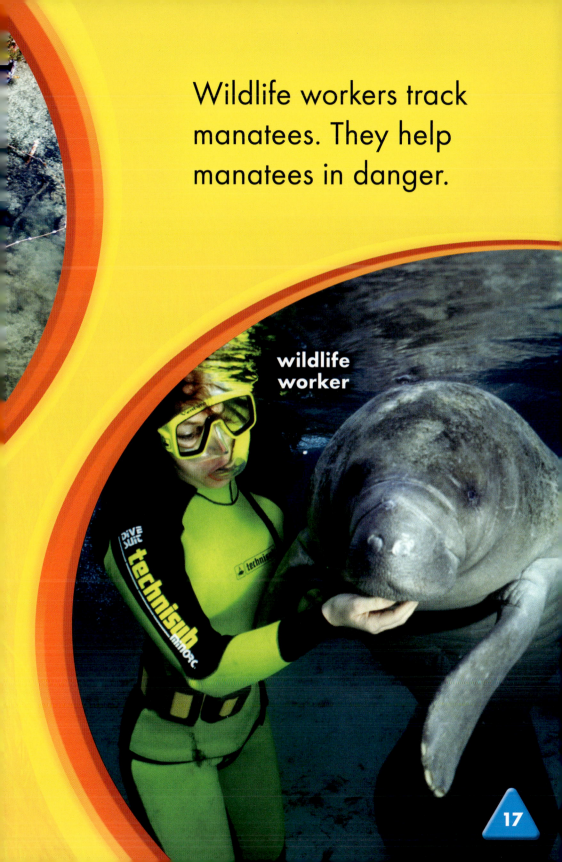

wildlife worker

Boaters can learn to look for manatees. They can slow down and pay attention.

People can be careful when fishing. They can stay away from manatees.

19

Everyone can help coastal waters stay clean. Using less plastic keeps trash out of oceans.

Adopting a manatee also helps save these gentle swimmers.

using reusable bottles

Glossary

adopting—taking over the care for someone or something; people who adopt wild animals give money for someone else to care for them.

climate change—a human-caused change in Earth's weather due to warming temperatures

habitats—places and natural surroundings in which plants or animals live

mammals—warm-blooded animals that have backbones and feed their young milk

mangroves—groups of trees and shrubs that grow along coastlines

pollution—substances that make nature dirty; pollution usually comes from humans.

protect—to keep safe

refuges—areas set aside as homes for wild animals

shallow—not deep

species—kinds of animals

To Learn More

AT THE LIBRARY
Chanez, Katie. *Manatees*. Mendota Heights, Minn.: Apex, 2021.

Riggs, Kate. *Manatees*. Mankato, Minn.: The Creative Company, 2023.

Schuh, Mari. *Manatees*. Mankato, Minn.: Amicus, 2021.

ON THE WEB

FACTSURFER

Factsurfer.com gives you a safe, fun way to find more information.

1. Go to www.factsurfer.com.

2. Enter "manatees" into the search box and click 🔍.

3. Select your book cover to see a list of related content.

Index

adopting, 20
boats, 10, 18
bodies, 4
climate change, 9
coasts, 6, 8, 14, 20
eat, 9, 10, 12
fishing, 10, 19
food, 6, 8, 9
governments, 16
habitats, 7, 12, 14
mammals, 4
mangroves, 6
noses, 4
people, 7, 8, 10, 14, 19
plants, 12, 14
plastic, 10, 20
pollution, 10
range, 7
refuges, 16
rivers, 6
seagrass, 8, 9, 12, 15

size, 4
species, 5
stats, 11
threats, 9
ways to help, 20
wetlands, 6
wildlife workers, 17
world with, 13

The images in this book are reproduced through the courtesy of: NaluPhoto, front cover; PHOTOOBJECT, p. 3; James R.D. Scott/ Getty Images, p. 4; Tsuneo Nakamura/ Volvox Inc/ Alamy Stock Photo, p. 5; Stephen Frink/ Getty Images, p. 6; George Wirt, p. 8 (top); trekandshoot, p. 8 (bottom); Ray Dukin, p. 9 (top left); Stephen Frink Collection/ Alamy Stock Photo, p. 9 (top right); Thierry Eidenweil, p. 9 (bottom); f11photo, p. 10; All Canada Photos/ Alamy Stock Photo, pp. 10-11; somdul, p. 12; Natalie11345, p. 13 (top left); pisitpong2017, p. 13 (top right); Microgen, p. 13 (bottom); ArteSub/ Alamy Stock Photo, p. 14; divedog, p. 15; Alex Couto, p. 16; Avalon. red/ Alamy Stock Photo, p. 17; B. Mete Uz/ Alamy Stock Photo, p. 18; ZUMA Press Inc/ Alamy Stock Photo, p. 19; Hanna Rusina, p. 20; David Fleetham/ Alamy Stock Photo, pp. 20-21; vkilikov, p. 22.

24